LEARNING

How to Walk

Inspiring Others to Walk by Faith

Cornelius Lindsey

Dedication

I would like to dedicate this book to a man who has chosen to live a life of faith and honor to our God. He has stepped out of himself, chosen to carry his cross, and truly follow the Lord in all He commands of him. He has chosen to abandon his own dreams, goals, and plans. His focus is sure. Carlis Howze, I salute you in your walk of faith. You are my brother and friend. I appreciate your life and all your contribution to the Body. Thank you for being my friend. This book is dedicated to your honor.

I would also like to mention the men and women around the world who choose to honor God. I salute men like Caleb Curl and women like Cierra Cotton who have chosen to abandon their own plans to live only as God directs them. There are so many others. I salute all of you.

Table of Contents

Introduction

Let's begin with a prayer. I want to pray for you as you prepare your mind to read the words of this book. Although the reading of the words is physical, I believe this book is spiritual in nature. I believe this book was written by the inspiration of the Holy Spirit. He inspires all words after times of prayer and reflection. I pray that you are challenged by what you read. It is my desire to encourage you to begin your life of faith or encourage you to continue the life of faith you have already started. Let's pray.

> *"Father, I ask You to bless Your child. I pray the words read are convicting unto repentance. Father, I know it is Your desire for those who do not know You to come to the knowledge of the truth. I know it is Your desire for men to be saved and set free from bondage to sin through Jesus. As Your child reads this book I pray You lead and guide him or her into*

all truth. Give clear instructions to Your child. Amen."

I truly hope you take in the words of that prayer. I also hope you make a decision to be fully obedient to whatever God asks of you as you read this book. If He tells you to move, move. If He commands you to speak to someone, speak. Do whatever He commands and do not hesitate. Hesitation is the breeding ground for faithlessness. Our faith will die the longer we hesitate on whether or not we should obey. You will lose your passion to continue forward the longer you hesitate. Obey quickly.

Throughout this book my prayer is for you to learn to walk by faith, not by sight, because "whatever is not of faith is sin," (Romans 14:23) and because "without faith it is impossible to please God" (Hebrews 11:6). You will discover the true meaning of faith and be encouraged to live out the words you will read. You will find out how walking by sight means we are leaning and trusting in worldly resources, human wisdom, our own sufficiency, and our ability to be self-led. Walking by faith means living in Jesus' wisdom, resources, sufficiency and guidance. We fully acknowledge we are not our own. We fully give ourselves to Him to be used for His service. We avail ourselves for His power, His direction, and His enablement. He is the teacher; we are the students. He speaks; we listen and obey. Walking by faith is an exciting adventure. It pushes us out of a sedentary life. It allows ordinary men and women to live extraordinary lives transcending the senses of this world by focusing on what he or she cannot see. It substantiates the realization that nothing about Christian life is boring.

The life of faith keeps the Christian man and woman on their knees seeking God in prayer so they can know the next step. It keeps them faithful in praising God and being thankful for all He has done. The life of faith is what God is calling all His children to do. Men are called to abandon their worldly pursuits to seek God by faith and fulfill all He desires of them. They are called to faith, not "Call of Duty." Women are called to the life of faith. They, too, are called to sacrifice and submit themselves under the direction of God. We are all called to please Him by faith.

There are many who preach about the importance of living by faith. Unfortunately, many of us are still led by sight. I know I have not spent all of my days walking by faith. I have many areas of my life where I continue to walk by sight. I can only imagine what I have missed out on because fear gripped my heart and caused me to remain stagnant, instead of moving forward in what I was commanded to do. I have passed people on the side of the road whom I know I was being compelled to minister to, but I felt my time was too important. There have been times where I was being compelled to give a certain amount of money to a stranger, but I did not do it because I was afraid of not having enough money for myself. I truly believe God compels us to walk by faith every second of our life. The key to our journey is being able to hear His voice and then moving when He compels us.

Many times my service, which includes my giving, is cut short because I do not want to be obedient or walk by faith. I have missed several opportunities of serving and giving because I was fearful. I have gotten so wrapped up trying to make things happen on my own. I tried to work harder to accomplish certain goals. I have tried to reach out to certain people thinking they would connect me to what I thought I wanted. I have sought to try to manage my own life and manipulate the things in my life so I could be in control.

My wife and I were preparing to move back to Georgia from Mississippi some years ago. We knew God was compelling us to move back. Unfortunately, our finances were not all there. Months before moving we had a good amount in our savings account for emergency situations; however, we had things to happen that required us to spend most of what we had saved. On the day I believe God told me us to move back to Georgia my wife came to and said, "Babe, I'm pregnant!" I was floored. It was a bit much to handle all at one time. Our truck was at the dealership because we needed a new transmission. That was not a cheap purchase. Then, we had to change the security system in the truck. After another costly expense, our emergency fund was depleting. Then, we got more news that my wife's job was not going to renew her contract. I was already self-employed. We were both preparing to step out in faith. In short, we would no longer have steady income through my wife's employment, our truck had very expensive repairs, we were moving from Mississippi to Georgia, and my wife was pregnant. All we could do from that point forward was trust God.

We searched long and hard for a place to live in the metro Atlanta area. I searched every website I could to find a place. One night while lying in the bed in Sweet Springs, Missouri, I was compelled by God to get up and search a housing site for a potential place to live. Upon pulling up the first page, we found a townhouse that was just perfect for us. It had everything we desired. Unfortunately, it was out of our price range. I knew it was meant to be the place where we would stay. I emailed the owners and told them our story. I wrote our story in the way I believe God desired. I used every word He gave me. I was at peace with the decision, and I felt like it would work out. I received an email from the owners about an hour after sending it. They were as ecstatic about us living in the home as we were. They wanted to meet us immediately and iron out all of the details. They were also open to lowering the price to something more beneficial to both parties. I looked back at that situation and cringe at all the long hours of driving around and looking at places. I wasted so much time trying to do things in my own way when all I needed to do was be patient, prayerful, and obedient. I am convinced we do not have to force God's will. We just have to walk in it.

I have preached so many messages about God's sovereignty, His power, His compassion, His guidance, His provision, His justice, and His faithfulness. However, I have not always practiced what I preached. I have had to question if I actually believed what I preached seeing how many of my days have been filled with stress, worry, fatigue, impatience, and desperation. Like all believers, I live with the constant struggle between fully trusting God or being sufficient in my own works. I have preached over and over again about God's ability and desire to lead us in the way we should go, but I have not always desired to be led. Let me be honest. There are times when I just want to quit and give up altogether. The criticism becomes too much. The heartache and loneliness is sometimes more than what I want to bear.

As a pastor I feel the heaviness of those who assemble with us. I feel their pain and hurts. I cry with them when a loved one dies. I celebrate with them at their weddings. I rejoice when they rejoice. However, my heart hurts when some choose to stray away. My heart hurts when some do not want to hear sound doctrine anymore. There are times when I desire God's perfect will for them more than they desire it for themselves. The heaviness only adds to the rationale in my head of why it is okay to quit and give up. It is a daily fight. We have temptation all around us, and we have every opportunity to quit and give up. We cannot afford to take it. We have to stop analyzing and scrutinizing every little detail. We must come to that place of trusting God at His word.

I had a young man ask me this question: "Cornelius, what made you step out in faith?" My answer to him was very thorough, and I will dedicate a chapter to that answer. However, the simple answer is this: "I honor God. When you truly honor God then YOU JUST DO IT!" If you overanalyze it, you will talk yourself out of it. When He speaks, you must obey—immediately. Do not put it off. Delayed obedience is still disobedience.

In this book, I chronicle many of my stories about walking by faith and I compare them with our son's experiences in learning how to walk. You will see the comparison in the walk of faith and the process of how toddlers learn to get up from the ground and walk. Watching my son learn how to walk has been an exciting experience, and the walk of faith is just as exciting. It is my prayer you will be encouraged to get up from the ground, stand boldly on your feet, and walk by faith. I firmly believe it is impossible to fail when you are consistently obedient to all God has commanded of you. It is time to walk by faith.

1

Learning How to Crawl

I will never forget the first time I saw my son crawl. I could see the desire in his eyes to move. He was desperate to get from one location to another without having his mom or me to carry him there. He got up on his hand and knees, gave us a stern look of determination, and crawled forward. My wife and I were so excited. He hit a big milestone that day.

Crawling is a big milestone for a baby. For those who do crawl before walking, it is their first way of getting around on their own. It is a major accomplishment. It was as big of an accomplishment for me when I started my crawl in my life of faith. Like my son, I had to be determined, but it was a slow and steady process. Like most children who begin to crawl I felt like I was moving backwards instead of going forwards most of the time. Crawling was a new experience for my son, and the beginning of my journey of faith was a new experience for me as well. It definitely took some time to get comfortable with it.

My walk of faith has not been ordinary. I look back over my life and I cannot help but think about all the things I have done in faith. I cannot help but think about all the places I have travelled, the stages I have been honored to preach on, the people I have been honored to meet, the family I have been honored to lead, and the list goes on. But, before all of those things happened, there was a moment in my life when I was deeply confused over my walk of faith. It happened in those beginning months after first hearing the Gospel. I was a sophomore in college. I heard messages on walking by faith and read a good amount of it in Scripture. It was like being told I could walk in a new way from how I had walked previously in my life. In fact, that is exactly what it is. But my beginning was not a true walk of faith; I was just learning how to crawl. Oddly enough, my crawling was just an adaption from being on my knees in prayer.

Praying to God was strange to me in those beginning months. I could not comprehend the idea of how a man of flesh and bone could communicate with the God who is not seen with the natural eye. I perceived it as foolishness, but I had a kind of conviction that only He could give to affirm that if I actually prayed to Him, He would answer me. I did not realize His answers were at His timing. I did not know in those beginning months there would be times of silence. I did not know there would be times of feeling hopeless. But, I was convinced He would eventually hear my cries to Him and answer me when I called. I had to learn that those who truly sought Him did it because they loved Him. Their motive was pure. And, they understand this principle: The act of seeking God is not bound by time limitations. This means they did not watch the clock or try to gauge how long they had been seeking Him. They just remained faithful in doing it.

When my son learned to crawl he started on his belly. I vividly remember him scooting back and forth on our hardwood floor. He was trying to move ahead, but his hands and feet were not in position. He had a look of determination, but he was not moving. After days of trying, he finally got up on his hands and knees. From there he would start crawling backwards. I thought it was the funniest thing. I could not understand why he was going backwards instead of moving forwards. It would seem that moving forward would be easier than moving backwards. However, I compared his moving backwards to the beginning of my walk of faith and I began to empathize with him. Although it looks easy to just move forward, it is not. It only took him about a week to change directions. All he needed was to go forward one time. My wife and I had our cameras out. We were excited. And one day he crawled. I was intrigued by it. I noticed he was able to truly crawl once he was in the right position. That observation meant so much to me because it was the same in my progression of faith. I, too, had to start on my knees, but my positioning on my knees was because I needed to be faithful in prayer. I needed to hear God instruct me. I needed to learn the value of the discipline of prayer. I needed to understand the importance of spending quality time with God. I needed to learn it for myself.

My understanding of God had to transcend the preacher's words and now jump from the pages of the Holy Scripture. He had to become more to me than an historical figure or an ideological character in a fiction novel. My understanding was that He was born of flesh, dwelt among us, took the wrath that was meant for our destruction, defeated death and the stronghold of sin, was buried, resurrected, ascended, and lives on to this day. He is my Lord, Jesus Christ. The beauty of His life is He has poured Himself out to those who believe as Romans 8:9 suggests. Because He pours Himself out for us, we have the ability to walk with Him. We have the ability to become one with Him. We go from being Christians to "Christ-Ones." This means we are in union with Him. This is why the disciples were able to go in His name and embody the same power He demonstrated in His own life. This is why demons trembled and obeyed His disciples when they went in His power and name. This is why we are able to call out to the Father. And this is the beauty of the Gospel.

I had to first understand the true significance of Jesus before I could grasp the concept of what it really means to walk by faith. He had to go from being my friend to being my Lord. I could not become so "friendly" with Him I lost all respect and reverence for Him. His significance had to be greater than anything I had ever ascribed to anyone else. It had to go beyond everything I could imagine with my natural mind. But, I knew I could not give Him that type of significance on my own. I had to be taught and enlightened to understand. My natural mind could not conceive His glory and magnificence. I needed Him to reveal Himself to me.

I have heard stories of people who were hit by big trucks going at a high rate of speed. Their bodies were forever changed because of the impact. There is no way a person would not be changed if they were hit by something that big at a rate of speed that could topple buildings. I have seen the damage on a truck after it hit a deer traveling very fast. The impact was so severe the deer was killed upon impact. I liken such an impact to my relationship with Christ. He has impacted me so powerfully I had to die. The difference between the deer and me is my death needed to happen so that I might live. Encountering Christ allowed for me to experience real change in my nature removing what was contrary to Him before I became alive in Him. It was that encounter with Christ that brought me to my knees. It was that encounter that put my face to the floor in reverence. It was that encounter that strengthened me to begin to move forward. It was the encounter that propelled my ability to crawl. And I started crawling.

One of my first small acts of faith was simply reading the Bible. Although I did not understand it, I was compelled to read it. I started reading the Book of John. I did not know at the time that it was written for unbelievers. Although I believed, I was new in my faith. The only thing separating me from the unbeliever was my belief. Unfortunately, my knowledge was extremely limited. John 16:13 reads *"But when he, the Spirit of truth, comes, he will guide you into all truth. He will not speak on his own; he will speak only what he hears and he will tell you what is yet to come."* It was because of this particular verse that a true desire arose within me to want to be taught by God the Spirit. I understand from that verse that He would guide me in all truth, and I knew that truth would be substantial and valid. Scriptures like 1 John 2: 20, 27 and John 14:26 helped me to understand the power and teaching ability of the Holy Spirit.

It was the power of Christ that enabled me to get on my knees. It was the understanding of Christ that kept me there. It was the leading and guidance of His Spirit that pushed me forward. He enabled me to crawl, and continuous obedience to Him strengthened my legs so I could stand firmly on my feet to walk.

Crawling is a very pivotal part of a baby's life. We must not forget there was a time in every mature believer's life when we could not take solid food. We were fed on the milk of God's Word. We needed simple truths that were easy enough for a baby to understand. Like a maturing being, we go through that same process with our faith. There is no reason why it should be overloaded with religious activity. I learned that it was okay to allow the Holy Spirit to lead me, guide me, and mature me. Like a good Father, it was like He grabbed me by my hand and walked with me. He was there at every test of my faith, and it was because of Him I was able to endure all of them. Crawling is nothing to be ashamed of for a believer who is compelled to walk by faith. We should not put time limits on how long one crawls before he walks. We are all different, and God reveals to each man in His own timing. So go ahead and crawl.

I would encourage you to begin by reading your Holy Bible. I love the American Standard Version. I do my best to stay away from any bibles that put more of an emphasis on watering down the potency of the Word to identify more with today's culture. The "thees" and "thous" can throw anyone off from time to time when reading, but rest assured, God teaches His children. He gives wisdom to those who ask of it from Him. In reading the Scriptures, ask questions, such as: Who is speaking? What is she/he saying? What is the location? Who is the audience? How does this relate to the Gospel? What is the Gospel? How can I clearly explain the Gospel to someone who does not know it? What does it mean to make disciples? How am I supposed to make disciples? What is a disciple? Etc. Questions like these helped me to understand the simple truths of the Word. They helped me to understand the basics. A baby does not start off in college. He must work his way up. As he matures, his lessons change. This is the progression from crawling to standing up to walking. You cannot crawl forever. The day will come when you will have no other choice but to stand up.

Standing Up On Your Own

I have had the opportunity and pleasure of walking by faith for many years. May of those years were lonely. God was with me, but people were not. For years I felt like I messed up or I was becoming too recluse. I tried to justify my being alone by saying I am introverted. I had never experienced anything like walking by faith before, so the idea that I needed to be without human influence was farfetched to me. I would try every opportunity I got to get around people and try to communicate to them the things God was saying to me. I would hold a bible study at my parent's home in an effort to share all God was saying to me and to have some kind of fellowship. Although the people heard what I was saying, they did not understand. They could not fully perceive every word I was saying partly because God had revealed those things to me, not them. I had to quickly learn I was privileged to hear His voice and be led by Him and it was dangerous to assume others would understand the things God said to me. I also had to understand He had to open my eyes to the truth. I did not open them on my own. In order for those around me to understand, they would have to have Him open their eyes. I could not do it for them. They would need to perceive the truth for themselves. They would need to know the walk of faith and understand all that goes in it.

My son started letting go of the edges of the couch and table to walk weeks before he chose to stand up on his feet when, moments before, he was sitting on the ground. He would crawl from one place to another, look at his mom or me for confirmation, and stand up on his own without any assistance from us. There were times in the beginning when his legs would shake and it would seem like he was going to tip to the front and fall. My wife and I wanted to assist him each step of the way, but we both knew that he had to learn how to stand up on his own without our assistance. We realized it was a new concept for him seeing he had been carried around for the entire first year of his life. He was going into a phase of development, but he had to learn the importance of standing up on his own without assistance.

In the same way, I had to learn the importance of standing up on my own when walking by faith. I could no longer lean on the admiration and acceptance of people. I could not rely on the approval or denial of man. I had to grow in full confidence with the Lord. I had to trust His leadings and not be moved by the absence of people in my life. The absence of people did not mean they were not around; it simply meant they were unable to connect with my journey. Have you ever been in a room full of people but still felt like you were by yourself? That is the feeling you have when you are in the company of others, but none of them understand how God is leading and guiding you. I felt that way for years. I would go hangout with friends and family, but I knew none of them truly understood the conviction God placed in my heart or the direction He was taking me. I felt like I could not be totally honest with them without facing persecution from them. This caused me to become recluse and closed off to many people. It led me to limit my interaction with others and reevaluate many of my relationships. Unfortunately, some of my friendships had to end. My focus was changing from hanging out and trying to have a good time to wanting to spend time in the Lord's presence and read His word. My focus changed from wanting to watch movies and shows on television to wanting to discuss truths within Scripture. My life and life of some of my friends were on two separate paths and going in two separate directions. Our paths needed to separate.

After moving back home after I dropped out of college I felt alone. I felt like no one really understood my position or knew what God was saying to me. In fact, it was wrong for me to assume they should understand what God was saying to me. He did not say it to them; He said it to me. I had to fight to stay true to what He said to me especially when I was persecuted by those who did not understand. First Corinthians 1:26-31 gave me comfort and strength. It reads: *"For consider your calling, brethren, that there were not many wise according to the flesh not many mighty, not many noble; but God has chosen the foolish things of the world to shame the wise, and God has chosen the weak things of the world to shame the things which are strong, and the base things of the world and the despised God has chosen, the things that are not, so that He may nullify the things that are, so that no man may boast before God. But by His doing you are in Christ Jesus, who became to us wisdom from God, and righteousness and sanctification, and redemption, so that, just as it is written, "LET HIM WHO BOASTS, BOAST IN THE LORD."* I love those verses. I found life in them because I felt like they spoke about my life. I am not considered wise according to our society. I do not have a college degree. In fact, I am college dropout. I have no titles or accolades to boast or brag about. I am lowborn and insignificant.

I was born in a small, country town in Mississippi. I grew up in a doublewide trailer with a pond in the backyard. I grew up with simple living—fishing out back to cook for supper. I grew up feeding calves and picking vegetables out of the garden. The only silver spoons in my house growing up tarnished after a couple washes. I also had a really bad stutter. I was terrified of speaking in front of people. I was overweight and very insecure. I hated to look at myself in the mirror and I had cried out to God so many times to just kill me that I have lost count.

By the world's standards, I am not mighty or noble. I was, and am, confident He chose me, one who is foolish to this world, to shame the wise. He did not choose me for my glory; He chose me for His. This is the same reason He chose you. There can be no pride in your understanding of this truth. His choosing you is by His will only. I had to fight against the part of me that wanted to prove my critics wrong. I finally realized how trying to prove my critics wrong would ultimately prove they were right all along. Trying to prove them wrong would show them I was concerned about their view of me and that I needed them to validate my success. I had to realize my success was not tied to their opinions; it is only about being obedient to God in everything.

Honestly, I did not ask for any of the stuff I do now. All I wanted was to know the truth and experience God for myself. I never asked to be a pastor. I never asked to travel the world to preach the Gospel. I never asked for the world I lived in for so long to be turned upside down. I never expected for all of my plans, dreams, ambitions, and goals to change. However, this is what happens when we submit ourselves fully to Christ. I cannot tell you how many people I have encountered who talk and sing about surrendering their all to God or withholding nothing from Him all while trying to maintain their lifestyle. They see Christian living as a short investment in a worship service or a minute of prayer over a greasy meal. I weep because they do not want to let everything go. They do not want to become foolish to the world so God can make them wise. They do not want to abandon their life so they are able to live anew in Christ. It is disheartening.

I have never made this portion of my life public in the way that I am about to make it now. My conversation with God concerning leaving college was one I have yet to shake or forget. Tears are welling up in my eyes as I write this. While on my knees in my apartment in Athens, Georgia God told me to never rely on man. Those words pierced my heart. I am not allowed to ever fully rely on man in any way. That reliance will make them believe they were responsible for anything good that has happened in my life.

Throughout the years I have cut off many relationships that threatened my promise with God. Those men sought to make me "their man." A man told me that he could make me the next big preacher. He flirted his affluence, influence and power, but I could not take his offer. It was a test of my faithfulness. I knew many men who would have taken the offer. They would not have thought twice about it. I, however, knew I could not. I knew I had to decline his offer and any offer like it. No man can claim any responsibility for all God has done for me. This part of my life—although very real—is difficult for me to explain. I have spent years trying to process it. Nevertheless, the greatest lesson I have gotten out of the entire experience is continued faithfulness to God over loyalty to man. There is nothing any man can give me that will ever top all God can do. There is no relationship on this earth that is more important than my relationship with Him. You must realize that truth as well. Without it, you will never truly be able to walk by faith. You will be bound in people bondage. There is no way you will be able to fully hear and obey the voice of God when you are relying more on the voice of man. You will lose friends. Some of your family will turn their backs on you. You may find more comfort with Christians you meet for the first time than you will with family you have known your entire life. You must remember the people closest to you "know" you. They know who you were in the past, and some will continue to judge you based on your past actions. They will be amongst the many who will have to watch you be successful in following the Lord. This is why it is important for you not to quit or give up. I have seen many of my family members come to know Christ because they watched my journey from the sidelines. Many of them have embraced the journey for themselves. Realize that you are not just doing this for yourself. Your walk is for God's glory, and it can be a wonderful testimony for many to see. So, stand up because it is time to walk.

Learning to Let Go

One of the greatest fears I have ever faced is of truly trusting God and others. I have oftentimes said I trust God, but my actions did not prove it. I would sing loudly with the rest of the congregation about my willingness to trust God at His word, but I would leave the meeting ready to follow my own ways. My trust was fickle and all talk. But I knew there was no way I could truly walk by faith without truly trusting God. And there was no way I could truly trust God until I finally let go of everything and everyone I thought I needed in my life.

The major hurdle and fear I faced when I was told to drop out of college was having to leave what was familiar. The educational progression of our society is daycare; then kindergarten; then elementary school; then middle school; then high school; then college. There are usually some post-graduate studies after the initial degree. I did not object to that progression. I felt like I was doing everything in the order it needed to be done. I felt I was right where I needed to be in my life. I was on the road to what I believed to be success. My goal was to graduate with a degree in Speech Communications and Political Science. I was contemplating enrolling in law school and practicing law until I made the decision to run for political office. That was my goal. I felt comfortable on campus. I felt comfortable being in the class. I felt like everything was going the way it was meant to go until I had my encounter with God. After that encounter I began to see things differently. It was like my eyes were opened to a whole new world I did not know existed.

After the encounter, I was not comfortable sitting in class. I desired to be in prayer. I had this feeling I needed to abandon my studies—if even for a few hours—to seek the Father. There would be times when I would go in prayer thinking I would be there for a few minutes. However, the minutes would turn to hours. There were times where the hours would turn to days. I would get so consumed in prayer that I did not want to leave. My dreams and aspirations quickly became secondary. They were not my focus. I wanted to know more of God, and I wanted to encounter Him like never before.

Because I spent so much time in prayer my friendships began to die away. There is an old principle I live by that I believe is full of truth: *Whatever you do not feed will eventually die.* Well, I was not feeding my friendships, and those relationships began to die away slowly. The reverse is also true: *Whatever you feed will eventually live.* I know that principle so well because it was the constant feeding of my faith that kept it alive. I have also experienced the reverse to the point I felt like my faith was on life support. It was barely alive. I would not feed it. Instead I would entertain friends and hanging out. I was more concerned about trying to be a good friend to men that I would neglect my time I once loved with God. Nevertheless, I found great joy in feeding my relationship with God and feeding on His Word. There would be days when I would ask Him to help me and instruct me to do more. I needed it in my life. I did not want to grow stagnate. I had to keep my faith alive and well.

Trusting God can seem very difficult because it is easier to trust in money, a career, an idea, a plan, a dream, parent's wishes, or any number of things this world says we should trust. It is easier to sing songs about trusting God and giving Him all of ourselves, but very seldom are those words ever lived out. I have told God many times He had all of me and I would withhold nothing from Him. The entire song was a lie. I was fully intended to withhold parts of my life from God. I felt like I needed to have that control. The pride in me did not want to break free and fully relinquish everything over to Him. That has been a constant battle in my life. Like many, I would sing and preach about my love for God, but, in all honesty, I did not trust Him enough to actually obey Him. My faith would mature each time I was obedient. I still have my days where I want to trust in my plans and give myself to my dreams, but there is a truth I cannot shake. At the heart of true obedience is the reverential fear of God and an unshaken trust in Him.

There is nothing or no one in this world who deserves my reverence like God. I oftentimes have to ask myself, "Who do I think I am?" What makes me think I have the right to war against or disobey the Holy God? Who am I to test Him at His Word? Is He not God all by Himself? My plans and dreams are merely piles of dust in comparison to the riches that await me in sacrifice and obedience. To try to hold on to the things I am familiar with instead of letting them go to be fully obedient to God is a slap in the face of every man and woman of faith who has gone before me. I had to realize I was putting a degree before God; exchanging political plans for His will.

When my son was beginning to walk he would grab the sturdiest object nearest to him so he could keep his balance and not fall. His legs were a bit shaky, but he was walking nonetheless. He just needed a little assistance. He had to learn to let go of what he thought was holding him up. He had to take his hands off of it and walk. As for me, I had to take my hands off my plans and walk by faith. The same goes for you. It is important for you to understand something so precious about walking by faith. When you let go of what was once holding you up you will notice that you feel more secure standing up than you did when you were leaning over on something. Those friends, that degree, the job, the money were a mere illusion, making you think you needed it in order to continue standing. You did not really need it. Instead you needed to let go and bind yourself to God without the possibility of being unraveled. This is true faith. It is binding faith. It is unshaken faith. It is the faith that says it is okay to let go.

Ultimately, the biggest reason many do not want to let go of what is familiar is because of the fear of the unknown. There is this mystic cloud that hangs around them and spooky music begins to play in their head. This is usually where the idea of faith becomes fantasy. This would seem strange especially since many actually believe God is real. How is it then that many believe He is real yet treat faith as if it is fantasy? It is not like I am putting my faith in a cartoon character. He is the living God; the Creator of all of creation. He lives. The problem comes in believing the lie that placing our faith in things and people is more real than placing our faith in God. All of the things of this earth will be ruined. It will be ultimately destroyed. In fact the things we see are all temporary and they are not as real as the things we cannot see. God, although I cannot see Him with my physical eyes, is real. The war we fight is spiritual in nature and it escapes the natural eye. This is why we are blessed all the more for believing even though we have not seen. Nevertheless, our major impediment to truly letting go is two-fold. On the one hand there is the fear of the unknown. But on the second, we want to know all the specifics.

I know I have fought this battle many times with God. I would hear God speak, but I wanted Him to give me all the specifics before I was obedient. I wanted Him to map out the entire journey so I could pick and choose which road I would take, what I would avoid, and what I wanted to experience. I would pray and fast for days for specifics until I realized one great truth: If I have all the specifics then there is no need for faith. Why have faith when I have all the specifics, right? Over time I had to learn some very important things in relation to walking by faith and being okay without knowing the specifics.

And it is wise for me to note I understand those who share this issue with me. I admit that I have a control problem. I want to know what is going on, how it is going on, why it is going on, when it is going on. I want to be in the loop in everything. I do not like sitting in a car unless I am the one driving. I want to be in the kitchen to see how my food is prepared. I just want to be in control.

The first thing you must understand is that walking by faith is a day-by-day process. When you walk, you will experience how His grace and mercy is new every morning. You will hunger for His daily bread. Everything you need for your journey will be provided for in that day. You do not have to worry about tomorrow or next week. Just be content and faithful in today.

Second, God's plans for you will not make sense to others. It also will not appeal to your human reasoning. I had to learn I could not base my walk of faith on my natural senses. I had to be led by God. For example, dropping out of college does not make sense, but it does make faith. There have been times when God has instructed me to give away my entire paycheck. That does not make sense, but it does make faith. You cannot live by your senses and be led by faith. You will have to choose one or the other. Just know that faith is what is required to please God. But His faith is what we need to continue walking with Him. There were many times when I would go to God telling Him why my actions did not make sense. Little did I realize that I was basically answering myself because my actions were not supposed to make sense; they were meant to make faith.

My question I asked God many times was "What is Your will for my life?" I had to learn that it was not the best question to ask. Instead, I should ask "What is Your will?" Based on 1 Timothy 2:4 we know that "God's will is for all men to be saved and to come to the knowledge of the truth." If that is His will then we should adjust accordingly. So often we are in search for something more specific before we truly understand the full picture. To know God's desire is for all men to be saved and come to knowledge of Him makes it easy to navigate when He speaks. Once I know His will it is fairly simple for me to know mine seeing that I am the servant submitted to Him. Therefore whatever He commands, I must do. So often we are looking for God to tell us to walk through a magic door and become a movie star. We want this fantasy that has been played out in our head time and time again to miraculously happen. If it does not, we try to make it happen on our own. That is when we find ourselves broken, dejected, and lost.

Another key element of walking by faith was realizing I needed to remove "me" out of the equation. If I am always the main idea, then there is a problem. I should not be the focal point; it should always be God and His will. It cannot be about my way and my thinking and my purpose and my this and that. It must be about Him. Removing me from the picture makes it more about Him and others than it does about me. I do not have to worry about myself, though, because I trust He will lead and guide me. When we truly find out what God is doing and what He desires to do it helps us know what He will do through us. When we know what He desires to do we do not have to waste time just doing something to pass the time away.

Finally letting go does not mean we lose something. It means we gain something so much greater. There was an old man who was waiting for a bus to stop so he could get on. While climbing the bus steps, one of his shoes popped off his foot and rolled outside. The old man walked to the back of the bus, took his other shoe off his foot, and he threw it out the window. A little girl who was seated on the bus noticed what the old man did. She walked over to him and asked, "Mister, why did you throw your shoe out the window?" The old man responded, "So whoever finds them both can use them." The old man understood something valuable about life. He was not interested in holding on to something just to have it. What good is one shoe if you do not have the other? The shoes would be of better use together than apart. The same is true about walking by faith. After you have abandoned your worldly endeavors and ungodly relationships it is time to just leave it all behind. There is no reason to hang on to something you have already lost. Do not try to keep something alive that should be dead. Walk by faith and be encouraged to let go. Like my son, let go of what you are leaning on. It is time to take your first step.

Taking My First Step

After hearing the Gospel preached, I inquired about knowing Christ more. I wanted a more in-depth understanding of the truth. I did not want to have a shallow grasp of the reality and existence of God. I needed something more than the elementary understanding of God. I wanted my faith to be solid and firmly rooted in something substantial. I wanted to know if what I heard about the Gospel was true. I wanted to know if the words I read and heard preached in church service were real. I wanted to live out the commands given to see if the Gospel I heard was worth following. I wanted God to speak to me. I wanted to encounter Him like Saul on the road to Damascus. I wanted to weep with passion for God's people like Nehemiah. I wanted to experience the continuous presence of God like David. I wanted to have the courage and faith of Joshua. I wanted to lead with honor like Moses. I needed to know that I was following a true, living God. My understanding of Him had to be deeper than anything I had ever experienced so my preaching would be truly convicting and real. At the time of hearing the Gospel, I immediately believed in the importance of sharing it with others. I wanted my preaching to be based on experience because a man who has had an experience is never at the mercy of a man who only has an argument. Intellectualism could not guide my understanding. I had to experience Him.

My first real step in my journey of faith was when I dropped out of college. It was not an easy decision. I felt as if I had a lot on the line. Throughout high school I prided myself on being an overachiever. I excelled academically and in all of my extracurricular activities. Once I arrived at college it was no different. I quickly became president of my community council and a freshman leader in the Student Government Association. From there I went on to win an election to become a senator with the Student Government Association. My win was significant because I was a sophomore who defeated many upperclassmen, I was a minority on a predominantly Caucasian campus, and I was affiliated with a political party that lost the election. Out of all the candidates in our political party, only two of us won. I was one of those two. I was truly on top of the world, but there was no doubt I was still empty inside.

Months after winning the election I heard the convicting message of Christ. After hearing the sermon I was convicted unto repentance. My eyes were opened to the truth and the sin I loved was brought before my eyes. The Light truly exposed my darkness. My desires began to change months after my encounter with Christ. I no longer wanted to climb the political ladder or try to become a leading political advocate on my campus. My view towards school even began to change. Although I loved learning, I could not help but think I was wasting my time. I was not wasting it because I was enrolled in college. I was wasting it because I knew I had not sought the Father inquiring of Him as to what I should with my life. I finally made the decision to postpone everything so I could seek Him and get direction for my life. During that time I was also hungry to hear Him speak to me. I wanted and needed that experience in my life.

I needed to put everything on hold because I was starting a different chapter in my life. I was learning how to walk again. This time my walking was different from before. Before hearing the Gospel I was led by my sinful desires. I followed the path I thought was right. I was following the sinful passions of my heart. After being reborn in Christ I needed to learn how to walk in the right way.

As a father I get to see a lot of similarities in my learning how to walk by faith compared to my son learning how to walk. Neither one of us did it before. When my son was learning how to walk he would cautiously hold onto the edge of something. When he let go he would fall down because he was off balance. There were times when the fear to let go was greater than the desire to walk.

Although I do not remember my transition from crawling to walking, I was able to relive it after God instructed me to leave college and turn away from the path I chose for myself. I noticed the fear my son had from letting go and just starting to walk. I had that same fear. There I was on my apartment floor crying out to God to speak to me after praying for hours. The day turned to night and I was still there. At the right time God spoke and told me to leave. After telling me to leave I put my head down and told Him I could not obey Him. I could not just "up and leave" college. I was thinking about what everyone would thing of me. I did not want to ruin my name. I immediately felt His presence leave me. I knew my disobedience grieved Him. I could not continue to grieve Him, so I immediately told Him I would obey. I was definitely afraid to let go of everything that was familiar to me. I did not want to let go, but I knew letting go was important to moving forward.

The next day I ended my lease to my apartment, packed all of my stuff up, and I went back to my parent's home. I was leaving everything I knew. All I had at that point was a word from God. I cannot show a word from God. It is not tangible for the world to see or to show for evidence. I would have people ask me to prove what I heard from God as if I could pull out a ticket stub to verify my time in prayer with Him. What they did not realize was my willingness to drop out of college was my proof. Noah was able to show a finished ark in the middle of a flood as proof he heard from God. Joseph had bread in the midst of a famine in Egypt to show that he heard from God. At the time of dropping out of college, I did not have anything except an unwavering trust. My faith was my proof, and my faith was proven by my actions. What I had might not have been much, but it was worth it to me. It was a heavy price I was willing to pay. That situation taught me a lot about walking by faith and being willing to take my first step. I learned that everyone would not support me. Those who would support me were apprehensive. Many would only believe after they saw some proof of success. And I learned I could not be held in bondage to their opinions of me.

After dropping out of college, I had many who told me I was crazy. A teacher asked me about my contingency plan for failure. With confidence in my voice I responded, "I do not have a contingency plan for failure because, with my God, I am not planning to fail." I had a local elected official at the time ask me what was my plan B and C and D just in case plan A did not work. What she did not realize was my plan A was not a normal plan. He is the creator of all mankind. Words cannot fully describe His majesty. He has proven Himself time and time again from the beginning of time. In fact, He is so powerful that time obeys Him. I was safe in placing my full trust in Him and allowing Him to dictate my path. I had to be clear in my explaining to her He was not just my plan A; He was my only plan. I gave up all other options to fully follow His way. I was His servant. I had friends who abandoned me because they felt like I was crazy and overly religious. I was told I was "so heavenly-minded that I was no earthly good." Well, I would rather be "so heavenly-minded and no earthly good" than "so earthly-minded that I am no heavenly good." Although their absence was felt I could not allow it to break me. I had to learn the valuable lesson of being content with God alone. And it was in that alone time I realized just how much God truly meant to me. I really never understood how God was all I really needed until I looked around and He was all I really had.

They also wanted to see proof of my obedience. They wanted to be there to hear God say to them what He said to me. God has spoken to me a lot over the years and I have learned a valuable lesson in hearing Him and not trying to show proof of Him speaking. For me, the proof was in my willingness to walk. For them, they needed a sign. They needed to see the bush set on fire. They needed to see Jesus stand before them with holes in His wrists and feet. They needed to be stricken with blindness and given sight again on the third day. They needed proof because they lacked the firm element of faith for themselves. I had to learn I could not validate God's words to me. All I could do was continue to live them out so others could see my actions based on my faith. I could not expect them to truly understand my willingness to walk by faith and obey God when He told me to drop out of college. I was living out and on this simple truth: He told me, not them! I could not expect for someone to understand what God said to me, and I could not expect for a carnal mind to understand spiritual truths.

I finally realized my definition of success was different from most of the people I was around at the time. I grew up thinking success was measured by what I acquired, the position I gained, the degree I sought after, the money I earned, the stuff I bought, the house I lived in, the car I drove. I always thought success was about the way I looked and the position I found for myself in life. After encountering Christ and renewing my mind the Holy Spirit began to teach me about true success. Success throughout Scripture is defined as obedience. Abraham was successful because He was obedient. The same was true for Joshua, Noah, Paul, David, Elijah, and the list goes on. Their success was not measured in what they acquired because we who are in God's company know we have acquired more than we will ever need when He has beckoned us to Him. There is not a car, house, boat, or savings account that could take the place of God. All of these earthly toys will turn to dust. I had to quickly learn I was not leaving behind anything I really needed. I had to become content with walking with God and taking my first step. It was not easy, but it has been worth it. Ultimately, you must understand that your actions prove your beliefs. If God has spoken to you, then act on it in faith. Let your actions be your proof that He has spoken, and He will remain faithful to fulfill His promises as he has spoken them to you. Just stay faithful and keep putting one foot in front of the other.

One Foot In Front of the Other

Our son quickly learned a valuable lesson in walking. You will get to each destination the same way—by putting one foot in front of the other. Walking is an act of progression. One must be actively doing it in order for it to be considered "walking." If he is not walking then it is safe to assume he is still. It is also wise to point out that one who walks must have a destination in mind of where he is going. We do not usually walk without having a goal in mind. There are some instances where walking is just a means to an end, but there is still some goal in those situations. My wife and I like to go to the park and walk while conversing. Our goal is not time or speed—it is simply walking together and enjoying one another's company. Walking, in that situation, becomes more of a method to support a greater goal—which is communication. Nevertheless, it has purpose.

It is wise for us to consider the purpose behind why we are walking by faith. Based on Hebrews 11, we know we do not please God without faith. We also know it is by faith and grace that we are saved through Jesus Christ. Our walk of faith is simply an outward manifestation of our inward confession. When I move when God says to move, even though I do not understand, I am outwardly showing I truly trust Him enough to obey Him. The walk of faith is never purposeless. It is never without substance. It always takes a person to a desired goal and brings them to a place of spiritual maturity. We will get tired while walking just like how I get tired when I have to take long walks somewhere. There will be moments when you feel like giving up is the best option. I have felt like giving up for years but I have to constantly ask myself: What is the other option? What would I be giving up to go back to living the way I felt was right and following my own plans—which included a college degree, a successful career as an attorney, and elected to public office? My answers to those questions quicken me to keep moving forward and endure until the end. There will be moments when the things you walk past look more appealing than the goal you are walking towards. It is in those times when you must stay focused and keep your eyes on Christ. When we walk by faith and seek to please Him we know our attaining goal is eternal life with Him.

As a believer I do not think there is a more pleasing life than that of walking by faith. I do not think we can possibly live to our fullest potential without walking by faith. We will always be limited by our natural senses if we only choose to focus on everything that is right before our eyes. Walking by faith goes deeper than anything that is natural. It is unreasonable for someone to make another step without really knowing what is going to happen. This is why it is nearly impossible for a carnal-minded man to really understand what it means to walk by faith. It takes faith to pack up your entire house and move to a different state just because of a command giving in a time of private prayer. I know it does because my wife and I did it. It does not make sense to the carnal mind. I know it does not. I had people who told me it did not make sense; however, it was not an option for me. After my wife and I were married we moved five times between two different states in two years. Some said we were confused as to where we needed to go. We did not see it that way. Each place we moved to offered something different we needed. Those places also allowed us to help those who needed it as well. We were truly sojourners.

It is deception for a preacher to tell a new believer Christ only offers comfort in this life. My years of being transformed by Christ have been full of being uncomfortable. On our third move, we moved into a house that was very old. The landlords were trying to put someone in it for quite awhile. It had a lot of issues. My wife and I toured the house with the landlord, and we both had peace about it. After a time of prayer, we both knew it was the house we were supposed to move in after our last lease ended. By looking at the house it was not our style, but we felt inclined to move in. After moving in we had many problems with the house, but we learned a very valuable lesson of being content. We started getting things fixed and really beautifying the home. After our time was up there we knew we were able to leave the house in a better condition than how it was leased to us. In fact, there was a new tenant to move in right after we left. We believed our job was to help the owners of the home and keep it up until the rightful person came along to live in it. That was our assignment. It was not easy or beautiful, but we wanted to be obedient. It required sacrifice, but that is the cost for true obedience.

We have had many horrific moving stories, but none really comes close to our first move after we were married. I was working for a church at the time we got married, but my days of working there were coming to an end. After I resigned I was told by God to move to Jackson, Mississippi. My wife and I did not really know anyone there. I am born in Mississippi, but I was born in a very small, rural town. Nevertheless, I was not close to my family there. I also had family in Jackson, but I was not close to them either. My wife's family is mostly in Michigan, and my immediate family lives in Georgia. Moving to Mississippi would mean that we were both going to be alone— but together. We ended up moving to Mississippi a couple months after resigning from my job. The night we packed up our two-story house was horrendous. It rained the entire night, and my so-called "friends" were anything but helpful. After hours and hours of packing we felt like most of it was on the truck that was meant to go. Unfortunately, I was the driver of the truck, and I literally hate driving big trucks. Even though I did not want to do it I had to realize a key piece of wisdom I learned from over the years: *Just keep taking another step even though you do not feel like it.* You will eventually get to your goal. But a man who stays still and complains or makes excuses will prolong the journey he will eventually have to make. We finally made it to Mississippi after a very long seven-hour drive. We pulled up to our new place that we had not seen or been in before. See, my wife and I had faith that God would lead us in the direction we were meant to go. I drove out to Jackson, Mississippi once before to view the territory. I wanted to go see the "giants" per say like that of Joshua and Caleb. While out there I did not find a place I had peace about living. As the day got closer for us to move, the search for a place intensified. My wife and I were arguing more and we were beginning to doubt. This was the first time my wife and I ever had to walk by faith as a couple. We had each done it individually, but there is a big difference in doing it when you are single verses being married. After my time of morning prayer, I was commanded by God to go to the internet to look up potential places to live. I felt like I struck gold. We found a great apartment in the downtown area that was about our price range. We ended up calling them that day, filling out the paperwork, faxing it back over, and paying the deposit online. All we had to show for our "new place" were a couple of online pictures. We would joke that we were about to live in an empty warehouse somewhere. People around us thought we were absolutely crazy and not in our right mind. I would agree with that a little. I would like to think that we were walking by faith with the mind of Christ.

After pulling up to the building I got out of the truck to look at the new place for the first time. The place did look like the pictures online. It was in a great area, and we were where we thought we needed to be—downtown. There was only one big problem. My wife and I moved from a two-story house with three bedrooms, three bathrooms, a bonus room, and so much more. We had a lot of stuff. The problem was that we were moving into a very compact loft that was about three times smaller than the house. We definitely had more stuff than we had space, so we did what anyone walking by faith would have done. We started giving stuff away. Like the man with the lost shoe in the previous chapter, we knew giving stuff away would serve a greater purpose. We knew it was time to just let the stuff go. The people who were helping us move walked away with a lot of furniture, clothes, food, etc. My wife and I knew that we were in for an awakening once we moved, but really never expected to go through some of the things we experienced. It was definitely a walk of faith we would never forget. I want to share some of those things with you now.

First, we had to learn to be uncomfortable. Our Christian life was not made to be comfortable. In fact, we are to grow comfortable in being uncomfortable. We are called to endure and sacrifice. Our endurance is put to the test when our patience is tested. It is easy to endure when everything is going our way. We learn if our faith is really sure when life starts to get uncomfortable, people start to abandon us, things begin to fail us, our light begins to grow dim, etc. It is uncomfortable to wake up early on a cold morning to pray because God is beckoning us up to spend time with Him. It is not comfortable to fast and keep a joyful countenance when all we want to do is eat big bowls of sugary snacks and complain. It is not easy to give away things you feel like you need because someone else needs them more than you. It is not easy to turn away from temptation especially in those stressful and tense moments. Those things are not easy, but they are worth it.

My wife and I had to learn the lesson of being uncomfortable very quickly. It was not easy for us especially since we left a life that we both thought was comfortable. We did not realize that it was all an illusion. We were focused on what we could see, touch, feel and understand with our senses. We were not looking at our situation with eyes of faith. I feared if the words of a man I once respected would come true. He said to my wife and me, "You will be broke, divorced, and living with your parents in one year." His words were filled with hate, but I felt like his words could possibly come true. I just did not want to fail. Looking back, I am so glad we endured the tough road to get to the place we are now. We are able to do more, give more, and say more. Being uncomfortable was definitely worth it.

Second, we learned how to be content. I will speak at greater depth about why I resigned from my last job in the next chapter. I bring up my last job now because it really helps to paint the full reason as to why we needed to learn the lesson of being content. My wife and I were in the mindset that God's blessings were known by all the things He could give us. So we continued to go to God for what we wanted from Him. We did not seek Him for Him. He was our "sugar daddy" not our Heavenly Father. The greed for things and position would have led to our ruin. I knew the pride I had and being in a place where it was fed constantly would have been dangerous for me. It was only appropriate for us to leave. Greed clouds contentment.

Upon moving to Mississippi my wife and I learned to be content with what we had. Although we did not have all the space we once had, the friendships in the area, family nearby, or established connections, we had one another. Because we did not have two steady incomes coming in our home at the time we had to be content with living with less. That meant there were nights when we had to eat green peppers and brown rice because that was all we had. We had to sell things on eBay in order to pay our bills or give to those in need. We had to do what we had to do in order to get to remain obedient, but we were determined. Things we sold online mostly funded some of my first missions' trip to the Middle East and Ethiopia. And we really had to learn the value of being content when we had a miscarriage. It hit us very hard. It was almost unbearable. However, we had to grow beyond it. We had to trust God and truly be content.

Being content was a difficult lesson to learn, but it has helped us so much. We are no longer attached to the things we have. And the valuable lesson in that is: *Never hold on to something so tight that you cannot let go of it when you are told to let it go.* We also learned that we are truly able to enjoy things and serve people when we are set free from them. My wife and I are set free from the idolatry of money. That freedom allows us to make it our slave and use it as God directs. Bondage kills; freedom gives life. Escaping the bondage of people allowed us to be free in helping them—even those who hate us.

Finally, we learned the valuable lesson of obedience. I know you are probably thinking that this is a rather simple lesson to learn. And I agree with you that it is definitely easy; however, the lesson is as deep as it is wide. One would think that the lesson of obedience stops at the action, but it does not. It is more than just performing something. It is about the heart. I can give to God all day long, but what is the condition of my heart? Am I truly giving because I love God and desire to obey Him, or am I giving because I want praise from others? We had to make sure our obedience was not clouded with ungodly motives. We had to make sure our hearts were pure. And we prayed to God to gives us pure hearts because we knew we could not do it ourselves. Our constant prayer was for God to search our hearts and burn out of us all those things that were not like Him. We earnestly desired to work out our own salvation with the leading and guidance of the Holy Spirit.

I will admit that the obedience is not easy. After hearing the message of Christ and fully engaging Him for myself, I desired to keep hearing the message preached. The only problem was the church I was attending at the time was about an hour and a half away from the college campus. My car was not the most reliable car either. I felt like God wanted me to be in a church service each time the doors opened. Plus, I felt like I could not devout more time to my studies than I did to hearing preaching. So I told myself that I would attend every Sunday morning and Wednesday night service. There were actually two services on Sunday morning, and I made sure I attended both of them. I made that almost two hour drive in Atlanta midday traffic to get there. Unfortunately, there would be times when I would not have money for food or gas. All I knew was that I made a pledge to myself to get there, and I just felt like God would honor it. I wanted to put Him to the test. There was one time when my car started smoking. It was running hot. I was in terrible rush-hour traffic, and I was going to be late for church. People were pulling beside me blowing their horns and trying to get my attention as if I did not see the big cloud of smoke coming up from under my hood. I was fearful, but hopeful. I sat in that car, turned up my praise music, and I prayed to God to get me to church safely. I know there were a lot of practical things I could have done. I could have just pulled over. I could called rescue or something to help. I could put water in the radiator or something. The list goes on and on. I just put my faith to work. Eventually, the car stopped smoking while I was praying and singing songs to God about His magnificence. You can call what I did what you want. I call it success because it worked. I drove straight to church and checked everything afterwards. Fortunately, everything checked out just fine. I got back to the college campus with no problems at all.

As I stated, there were times when I did not have money to buy food. I could have eaten on campus in the cafeteria, but I had to leave by a certain time in order to make it to church on time. Being late was just unacceptable. I could not wait for the cafeteria to open up. It was also during those times that I would not have money for gas. There were so many times I asked God to lead me to church. I would just ask Him to get to there. If the car quit there I would just walk back. I just needed to get there. God never abandoned me. After one service He instructed me to go stand in line and purchase the CD of the sermon. I knew it had to be God because I did not have a dime to my name. All I wanted to do was be obedient. As I got closer to the register I felt such peace. I was not nervous at all. I was next in line when a gentleman standing behind me tapped me on the shoulder. He asked me to step out for a moment so he could speak with me. He told me God told him to pay for my CD for the service that evening and to give me a gift. He held out his hand and he had a wad of cash in it. I had enough to buy the CD, get gas, and get food. I did not eat like a king, but I did not starve like a pauper either. God proved His faithfulness. He also proved that He would honor those who chose to honor Him.

Each step of obedience we took taught us a different lesson, and those lessons still stick with us today. I have said it before and I will say it again—I could not have learned these valuable lessons in such depth in a classroom. I could read about the walks of faith by other men and women but experiencing it for myself was more than I had ever imagined it would be. Be encouraged to take that next step of faith. Do not live with the fear that the next step is too big a step to take. That is a lie. No step is too big to take. Stay focused and take it. It is my prayer that you have been encouraged so far and that you are encouraged by the next chapter where I go in some detail about getting up when you have fallen down.

Getting Up When You Have Fallen Down

Our son has had his fair share of falling down after he took a couple steps when he was learning how to walk. We could tell he was becoming frustrated. He walked with such passion. It was like he wanted to take off running. Unfortunately, he would lose his balance and fall down. From there, he was tempted to crawl again. There would be times when he chose to stand back up on his feet to start again.

I have been in my son's shoes in more ways than one. I am sure I fell down when I started walking. I also know I fell down a lot when I started walking by faith. Like my son, I would lose my balance and fall down and falling down did not feel good.

I started preaching in 2009. At that time no one was interested in what I had to say. I would preach on a conference call line for an hour. People were not using conference call hotlines for things like that back then. Nevertheless, it was the method I choice for the time being. When I started out, I only had one person to call in to listen—my wife. She was faithful to listen even if she was mad at me. You know that is a big deal if you are married. God continued to tell me to record the sermons and He would not let me quit. I was so focused on the lack of audience. I looked at it as if I was failing. I would preach a general sermon on Sunday evenings. Then, God told me He wanted me to preach on relationships on Tuesday nights. I was very much against it seeing how I already felt like no one was tuning in. Nevertheless, I kept going. We went from a few people each week tuning in to thousands of downloads in one day. My wife and I were shocked by the number of people who chose to download our sermons. And the messages we received from people who were blessed by past sermons we preached when no one initially tuned in started pouring in from all over the world. It all became a lot at one time. Like in any endeavor, the compliments also brought a great deal of criticism. We had to quickly learn that if we chose to live on their compliments we would die from their criticism. We had to mature in this area very quickly.

Two years before TeleChurch—that was what we called the Sunday and Tuesday evening sermons—I had my own Christian radio show. I was full of enthusiasm, but I was ignorant of a lot of things. My faith stood taller than my wisdom. I knew I had a charge from God to preach His Gospel so I wanted to shout it from every rooftop I could find. My rooftop of choice just happened to be a radio show.

Unfortunately, I partnered with two young guys to join me on it. We called it "The Sons of Thunder Radio Show." The partnership did not last two days. They quickly backed out of the deal, and I was left there with the full payment and responsibility on my own. For clarity, I had already dropped out of college by this time. Overall, I could not maintain the show. I could not afford to pay for it, and I could not devote enough time to recording the sermons to be played. I knew I was in too far over my head. I also knew that God did not tell me to start the show. The only specific command He gave me around that time was: "Wait!" and "Be Patient!" My impatience and overzealous attitude took me off balance and I fell. Since it was one of my first times falling after I had started walking by faith, it really hurt. It was also very embarrassing.

Have you ever been out in public and tripped over something and fallen down? Well, I have. I will never forget what happened to me in what felt like one of the coldest nights in Manhattan. I was walking down Madison Avenue and I was fully determined to get back to my hotel quickly. I was looking straight ahead because I did not want to look anyone in the eyes. Unfortunately, I did not see the wide crack in the sidewalk. As I was walking I stepped right in the crack, tripped out of my shoe, and fell flat on the ground. There were people all around. I could hear the people laughing hysterically at me. I tried to laugh with them, but I was very embarrassed. I have tripped and fallen many times. I have always noticed the falls seem to hurt more when people are watching. The hurt is not necessarily from the fall as much as it is from the embarrassment that comes along with it. I was very embarrassed one afternoon when I fell multiple times while trying to ice skate. I tried to be Mr. Popularity and get everyone's attention so they could watch me skate from one end to the other. I did not make it off the wall before I fell hard on my side. The pain moved all through my body. It was not fun at all. I was very embarrassed. The embarrassment, plus the pain from the fall, was almost unbearable to handle. I wanted to just stay down on the ice and never get up again, but I knew the time would come for me to stand back up, face those who laughed at me, and move forward.

Honestly, I believe the embarrassment of the fall hurts more than the fall itself. After I fell on my walk of faith by making many bad decisions where I was not God-led, I had to deal with the embarrassment and criticism from others. The criticism was sometimes harsh and downright mean. I felt like it came from a place of anger and resentment from others. A lot of it was based in ignorance. Nonetheless, it was hurtful and damaging. I cried many times. It was painful. Falling on the ground was painful. Being on the ground was lonely. But, standing back up was important.

You are not a failure just because you fell down. You have officially failed if you refuse to get back up. Proverbs 24:16 reads: *"For a righteous man falls seven times, and rises again. But the wicked stumble in time of calamity."* It does not matter how many times you fall; what matters most is you getting back up again. We can really learn from our errors and failures. God is not keeping a total of your failures. God forgets when He forgives.

He casts your sins from the east to the west. There are consequences for our transgressions, but He still forgives us.

Look at Peter, one of Jesus' disciples. I love Matthew 14:28-30 when Jesus commanded Peter to get out of the boat and walk on the water and come toward Him. Many criticize Peter for taking his eyes off the Lord and beginning to sink. One of the things I think many of us miss is Peter's courage in actually getting out of the boat. Peter did sink though. He had several moments where he stood tall in defense of Jesus. However, one of his greatest fallings was when he denied Christ three times. He fell down hard. Unlike many men in that situation, Peter did not stay down. He got back up and served our Lord. Many would not attempt to get out of the boat. Many would have allowed fear to grip their heart and comfort to keep them from moving forward. Oftentimes, it is the fear in our heart and the desire to be comfortable and normal that keeps us afraid of moving forward.

Let go of the fear. Walk valiantly into the future knowing that Christ's Spirit abides in you. He has the power to cause the thunderous storms in your life to dissipate. He gives you peace that calms raging winds and stills the storm-tossed sea. If you just stay focused on Him you will not be caught off balance. I got distracted while trying to ice skate by being the center of attention. My distraction cost me dearly. I fell. I fell hard. Do not try to impress the spectators. Just stay focused. Do not look at the waves of the sea when Christ is beckoning you to get out of the boat. Get out! Step out of it! Go! Go! Go! Do it! Walk by faith!

I know you do not have all the answers. That is why it is faith. You cannot have both faith and the reason of this world. If you try to live with both, you will end up with neither. Go ahead. Make that phone call. Plan the meeting. Get everything in order. And remain in prayer through all of it. I pray grace, mercy, and peace for you as you continue this journey. Now, go ahead. Get back up. Do not concentrate on the vile, empty words of your criticizers. Just remain focused. Keep taking another step.

Stepping Out

Leaving college was the biggest decision I ever had to make. It was definitely a choice between obedience and disobedience. Looking at my life now, I am proud of the choice I made. Although it does not look like traditional success, it is obedience. And obedience always overrides the world's standard of success. I would not dare insinuate to others that their path should look exactly like mine. I do not think it is God's specific will for every man and woman to drop out of college as I did. In fact, I left college because I did not seek God about whether or not I should have enrolled. At the time of selecting a college my mind was focused on a young woman and a good career. I did not consider God at any time. If I would have had the same convictions then that I do now, I would not have had to drop out. However, there was no way God could beckon me to Him and I not drop everything. I had to answer His call. And although dropping out of college was a big deal, it was not my only walk of faith.

Years ago I was flying over to the Middle East for the second time with a group of men. We were excited about traveling there and sharing the Gospel of Christ. Although I was excited my heart and focus was elsewhere. Weeks before traveling there, God had been dealing with me about traveling to Ethiopia. I had never been to Africa before. I was excited and nervous. All I had was a word from God. I did not know anyone there. I had no connections at all. I was going to be alone in another continent with people I did not know. I had another big problem. I did not have the finances to get there. I had just enough to get to the Middle East, and I had a little spending money. I felt like all the past times I trusted in the Lord brought me great results. I could not think of any reason why this time would be any different. He never let me down then. I had no reason to believe He would let me down with this trip either.

As the time slowly approached for me to fly over to the Middle East I intensified my times of prayer. I knew I was preparing to go into a battle that could not be won with words alone. I had to invoke a special kind of power through consistent prayer that would prepare the way for me to go and set the course to ministering to the lost when I landed. After spending a couple days in the Middle East I was preparing myself to travel to Ethiopia. The ticket purchased for me was charged, and I was supposed to pay the person back. Unfortunately, I did not have the money. My wife and I went to our closet and took out everything we thought had value. We uploaded pictures of it to eBay so we could sell it and use the funds to support the mission to Ethiopia. We also wanted to use the funds to help an orphanage I found out was located along the outskirts of Addis Abba, Ethiopia. I sold every watch I had. I put up my jeans, bags, shoes, shirts, ties, and suits, to try to get as much money as I could so I would have enough when I got there. Nevertheless, there I was in the Middle East and the day arrived for me to tell our friend that I did not have the money to pay for my flight. I will never forget that day for as long as I live.

I woke up early that morning to pray and I was given so much peace. After prayer God told me to go to one of the local malls there in Dubai. After I arrived He would give me the next set of instructions. You must understand, I did not have any method of communication with anyone except a wireless connection in the lobby of our hotel. I got dressed, prepared myself, and I took a taxi over to the mall. It felt like the day started to get progressively worse. The new camera I was gifted to take on the trip broke when one of the guys dropped it. I was only able to use it one time. I figured I would take the camera over to the mall to see if anyone could fix it for me. The weather was extremely hot. I was sweating profusely. The taxi driver drove me in circles before finally getting me to the mall. After arriving there I did not know the first place to start or what floor to walk first. I figured I would find a store that could fix my camera.

After nearly an hour of trying to get the camera fixed, I was told I would have to buy a new one. There was literally no hope for it. I walked out of the store defeated, and I still had the cloud of doubt over my head that I would not have the money to pay for my ticket to Ethiopia. I decided it was best to just give up, go back to the hotel, and crawl in bed. I felt like I possibly missed God. While walking out of the mall I heard God tell me to go to the bottom level of the mall and walk straight. Feeling defeated and set in my own pity party, I wanted to disobey Him, but I figured it would not hurt anything for me to go down and walk. I got down to the bottom level of the mall and I started to walk straight. I did not know what I was supposed to look for or see. All I knew was this principle: *Faith is being able to walk in accordance to what you have been commanded without having all the details.* And I did not have all the details. As I walked through the bottom level I started to pass by kiosks filled with merchandise. The mall was crowded with people. I felt like I was trying to find a needle in a haystack. Nevertheless, I walked forward. After walking for about ten minutes I noticed the hair of someone my wife and I knew who lived in Dubai. I called out the person's name, and indeed, it was she. We exchanged small talk for a minute. Then, she told me that God told her to come down to the bottom level of the mall. She did not know why she was going down there. It was at that moment my faith was filled. She looked at me with tears in her eyes and said, "Cornelius, God told me to give you this. He told me to tell you not to worry about your ticket to Ethiopia. I am going to pay for it." Those words gave me so much relief. My knees started to shake and I was overjoyed and overcome with emotions. It was at that moment I realized something about the walk of faith that is so vital for all of us to understand: *If my obedience can bless someone then my disobedience can hinder him or her.* I started to wonder what would have happened if she chose to disobey God and not obey Him when He told her to meet me. What would have happened if she did not obey Him when He told her to gift me the money? That one act of obedience impacted me more than an hour-long sermon.

Well, I got the money from her, and I stepped foot on the plane to Ethiopia the next morning. I was excited but nervous. I knew God would make a way for me. I knew He was with me. He had proven Himself time and time again. The only issues I faced at the time was that I was alone. Yes, God was with me, but I did not have any physical companionship. Also, I did not have money to really stay in Ethiopia. All I had was $100, and it was supposed to last me for five days. After landing in Ethiopia I had a driver and the mother of a young man I knew who lived in Mississippi to take me to my guesthouse. It was a complete culture shock for me. I did not have a phone or Internet, so there was no way of telling my wife that I was okay. I was literally out walking by faith by myself.

Upon landing I was immediately reminded of the entire chapter of Luke 6. Specifically, I was reminded of the charge Jesus gave to His disciples to deny themselves, take up their cross, and follow Him. I was also reminded to go into the world and believe He would be with me. I was fully prepared to go to a person's house and hope they received me in their home. If not, I would dust my feet off and tell them they rejected me and the One who sent me. Fortunately for me, I was not rejected. I was taken to a guestroom at someone's home. The room was located above a big enclosure where the biggest dog I had ever seen was living. His name was Shark. They called him Shark because he had teeth like a shark, and he was trained to protect their yard. His bark was thunderous. Underneath my bed was a machete that was supposed to be used just in case someone attempted to come in the room. I did not understand the native language, so I did not find much interest in what was on television. I spent that first night in prayer and reading Scripture. I could not believe I was actually there at the place God told me to go.

I spent my mornings in deep prayer and sitting with the locals. It was definitely an exciting time. While there I met a family who accepted me as their own. They allowed me to stay in their house, eat at their table, and sit with them in the evenings. We had special times of prayer and encouragement. I felt like I was able to minister to every person in the family individually. I was also honored to meet a man who I am still friends with to this day. He is a pastor of a church located in Addis Ababa. He also believes in preaching the true Gospel of Christ.

After our first introduction our souls were knit together. God really connected us as friends. He invited me to preach at his church on two occasions while I was in Ethiopia, and you better believe I preached. After preaching in the church I was led to start praying for people in their homes. It was truly powerful experience. I went from house to house praying for families and communities. I prayed over the disabled and sick in hopes they would recover. I prayed for God's perfect will to be done. I anointed doorposts with oil and prayed over the doors leading into their homes. I knew I was on a mission, and I was not going to allow anything to stop it.

After full days of prayer I would be exhausted and needing to be refreshed in my own time of prayer and fasting. But, before leaving I wanted to see the orphans I traveled so far to see. On the day before my departure back to America I had the opportunity to go to the orphanage. The day before going I asked God to allow me the opportunity to give them some more money for the orphanage even if it was not much. After preaching my final sermon at my friend's church he handed me an envelope filled with money.

I gave that money to the orphanage the next day, and they were so excited. The amount of money I gave them was exactly what they needed. Again, I had to ask myself the questions: What if I did not go? What if I chose not to be obedient? What if I gave up? Who would have suffered the consequences of my disobedience? I finally got back home and that journey was complete.

I look back on it I am so glad I did not disobey God. Stepping out in faith taught me so much about what I had read in the Scripture that I would not have gotten in a classroom. It was in Ethiopia that God began to show me the truth and accuracy of Scripture by confirming many things to me. It was there I realized and was able to see with my own eyes the correlation between a shepherd and his sheep. I was able to look at the difference of a mustard seed and a mountain and compare the two as Jesus did in His teachings to the disciples.

It was there I was able to devout myself and give full attention to the Lord without having to perform any other duties. It was there I was able to recklessly abandon any image I had built of myself and be around people who only knew me as a young preacher who was willing to obey God. I did not set out to preach, but experiences like this one filled me with passion. So much so that I had to tell the world about the glory, righteousness, and faithfulness of my God. These experiences propelled my faith and encouraged me to continue my walk. There is a world of adventure out there for you. There is so much to experience. Do not waste your life away performing mundane activities that serve no eternal purpose. Be mature enough to walk by faith instead of watching others from the sidelines.

Walking Versus Watching: Experience Versus Knowledge

When my son took his first step I was on the couch watching. I was there when he let go of the coffee table and started walking with confidence in his eyes towards his mother. My heart filled with joy and a smile was painted on my face. I was one excited daddy. There was a big difference between my and my son's experiences. I was merely watching him; he was actually walking.

I have spent many years walking by faith, and I have been able to experience both walking and watching. I gained so much from both experiences. From walking, I was able to gain experience, and no one can take experience away from me. A man with experience is never at the mercy of a man with an argument. The man with an argument is usually the one who has never actually experienced what he's arguing. His argument is built on knowledge he has heard or read. The man with experience is able to take the knowledge he has received and tests it against what he has experienced. The man with experience is able to preach and teach with passion because his understanding is deeper than the words found on paper. The man with knowledge is limited to what he has learned from either reading or hearing. As I stated in previous chapters, I did not want my Christian experience to be a sum total of what I heard from preachers. I needed to experience Christ for myself. I needed to know what it felt like to hear the voice of God, to walk by faith, and be willing to remain faithful to all He asked me to do.

While in middle school I played football. I must admit I was not that good. I did not really understand the sport, and I still do not understand it. The positions I played were fairly simple. At one point I was a left tackle. My job was to block. I also played the role of a center. My job was to make sure the quarterback received the ball. That was my limited understanding of the game, and I would like to think I did well seeing how I did not really understand it. Nevertheless, there would be times when the plays the coach called on the sideline did not go as planned on the field. The coach would get so upset the only three hairs on the top of his head stood straight up. He wanted the plays to go as practiced. The only difference was that during practice we did not have an opposing team of angry boys looking to stop us on every play. I would get so frustrated because I noticed a difference in position between us--the players--and our coach. We were actually involved in the game. We were players. He was merely watching from sideline and calling out different plays. I felt like he did not really understand the situation on the field because he was not on it; he was on the sidelines. Our coach was not an active player on the field but it was reassuring to know he had been there before. I had to have the right perspective. It was the people in the stands who did not properly understand the intensity of the game on the field."

There would be times where many spectators would come up to us after a game to interject their opinion about the way we played. They had their own view of what we should have done, how we should have ran, who we should have hit, etc. I am not dismissing their knowledge, but I want to make sure it is in the proper perspective. They were in the stands watching the game; we were actively playing in it on the field. The experience is totally different. I have had the pleasure of being on the field and in the stands. While in the stands I did not have anyone charging at me in full pads trying to run me over. There was a level of safety in the stands, and I did not feel at risk or under any pressure. Well, I guess the only pressure I felt was wanting to make sure I did not waste any ketchup on my clothes while I tried to eat my hotdog. I had a sense of pride while being in the stands because I felt like my view helped me to know things that were not noticeable when playing on the field. I could see the mistakes, the misses, the hard hits, and the beautiful catches from the stands. It was easy for me to call out plays and scream at the team for an awful play. It was easy to do it from the stands because I was not under pressure like I have been on the field.

There is a different feeling while on the field. While on the field I have been under a great deal of pressure to make sure I performed accurately. I had to make sure the ball was in the right place, at the right time and that I blocked the right man, at the right time. I had to remain focused on my job. I did not have the pleasure of being able to watch the entire field and know who was open, who was charging towards me, who was in jeopardy of being hit hard, or who was about to catch the ball. I had to focus under the pressure. Not only was I performing under pressure from my teammates, I was also performing under pressure from those in the audience. I knew I was being watched. While I did not make that a major concern, it was always in the back of my mind. I also knew the game was mine to lose if I did not perform my job accurately. I did not have that same pressure while sitting in the stands watching.

When I began my journey of walking by faith it was like I was stepping out on the field for the first time. I had the plays in the hand. I was familiar with my Coach—the Holy Spirit. I was ready to play. Well, I thought I was ready to play. What I did not account for were the many things that could happen because I stepped out in faith. There was an actual football game we played one year where a teammate of mine was so pumped up to get on the field. He knew his play. He was ready to perform it. I hiked the ball, the quarterback stepped back deep, threw the ball, and our teammate ran to catch it. When the ball fell into his arms, a player from the opposing team hit him hard. He hit him so hard that he shattered his collarbone. It was difficult to watch. Our teammate did not get to play football for the rest of the season. He was hurt and shaken up pretty bad over it. He was active in the game, but he never expected something like that to happen.

I know you may never have considered the walk of faith to be difficult. You probably thought you were going to be able to walk out on the field, know all the plays, run them perfectly without opposition, and score every time, right? Well, that is not going to happen. I have heard preachers lie to new coverts by telling them that the walk of faith and the life of a believer is without hardship. That is not true. The central theme of the New Testament is endurance and sacrifice. Notice the example of Christ. He endured to the end. Men like Paul and Peter endured to the end. They kept the faith. Like Christ, they were willing to sacrifice their lives for the purity of the Gospel. They faced opposition, but they did not quit.

I must admit I have had great joy in watching a few games, but there is no greater experience than actually participating in one. Taking the walk of faith means you are willing to come out the stands, get off the sideline, and step out on the field. It means you are willing to put on the whole armor of God and prepare for the opposition. And yes, there will be opposition. You will war a very real spiritual battle every step of the way. You will have to put away the controllers and stop playing simulated battles on "Call of Duty" in order to accept the true call of duty from our Lord and King. The enemy will do all he can to distract you from the path. He will infill you with so much fear it intoxicates you—which makes you double-minded and unstable in all your ways. And a double-minded man cannot walk the straight, narrow path. He will stumble and fall. Some do not ever get back up.

There have been times when I have felt like quitting and giving up. I have felt undeserving of God's direction because I constantly ran back to the sin I continued to profess to others I had grown to hate. I have spent hours in my bedroom closet contemplating suicide because I did not want to live any longer. I just wanted to die. I felt I had ruined my life by following God. I would listen to the voices of the people in the stands who would shout out to me, "Turn from God! Follow your own way! You are smarter than what you are showing to be, Cornelius!" They wanted to see results of my faith just like the audience wants to see points on the scoreboard. The points indicate whether or not their team is winning. Well, my points are spiritual in nature. I could not show them the points they were looking for. All I could do was continue playing in hopes, that by watching my life, they would be inspired to come on the field with me. I have felt the heaviness of depression and the weight of doubt. I know that spiritual war so well. I have felt the torment by the enemy as my dreams were infiltrated and I was being tortured in my sleep. I felt like I was not safe awake or in slumber. I have felt empty in times of prayer and totally wiped out after I have preached my heart out. I have felt the pain, agony, hardship, and weariness that comes with being active on the field. But, each time I get close to giving up the Holy Spirit strengthens me to go for another play. I am encouraged to endure and finish the race I started.

More than anything I have heard the shouts of doubt from those who have become content in watching my walk of faith. I have learned to really pray for them because I know they watch my walk because they do not have the faith to do it on their own. My prayer is they acquire the faith to walk on their own and finally let go. I have had to learn I cannot allow for their words to cripple me. If I live by their compliments, I will die from their criticism. I had to learn to stay focused on the action on the field. I could not give my attention to the pettiness taking place in the stands. 2 Timothy 2:4 reads "No soldier in active service entangles himself in the affairs of everyday life, so that he may please the one who enlisted him as a soldier." Therefore, there is no way I can be an effective soldier in God's army if I am constantly focused on the concerns, arguments, discussions, gossips, of those who choose to spectate. Trying to pay attention to both the field and the stands will make you double-minded and unstable, and you will fall.

The one thing I love about experience is it does not bow down to age. I have met men who were much older than me but their experience in walking by faith was far younger. Therefore, their preaching reflected their young experience. I have encouraged young men to get away with God and allow Him to speak. That could mean going out in the woods with nothing to just sit and pray until God speaks. I have sat out in the woods looking up at the top of the trees waiting for God to give me my next set of instructions. I wanted to hear Him, and I was willing to do whatever I had to do to hear Him. Go ahead and turn off your technology. Get in a closet and stay there until God breaks your heart and you begin to weep in desperation and yearn for Him like the fawn yearns for the breast of the doe. Have you ever been so hungry and thirsty for Him you were willing to cancel all your plans and abandon your life's pursuits just to sit in His presence? If not, what are you waiting for? Accept the call to deeper obedience! Although the road is narrow, there is still room for you to walk it. Many do not walk by faith in our day. They have grown content with watching from the stands. Do not let it that mindset describe you. Go to your knees in prayer, then go to your feet in obedience. Start walking and do not stop. Endure until the end.

Finding the Courage to Run

The progression of movement for a child is usually seen in crawling then walking then running. There are some children who skip one, if not two, of those steps. I have seen kids go straight from crawling to running, and they have not stopped running since. One thing I know about running is that it takes great faith.

I love how the Apostle Paul equates our Christian life to that of a race. Hebrews 12:1-3 reads "Therefore, since we have so great a cloud of witnesses surrounding us, let us also lay aside every encumbrance and sin which so easily entangles us, and let us run with endurance the race that is set before us, fixing our eyes on Jesus, the author and perfector of faith, who for the joy set before Him endured the cross, despising the shame, and has sat down at the right hand of the throne of God. For consider Him who has endured such hostility by sinners against Himself, so that you will not grow weary and lose heart." This life is like a big race, and we must not get weary when running it.

Running is about speed and accuracy. It is also about pace. While in high school I decided to join the cross-country track team. I was not a runner then and I am not a runner now. My involvement was to look well rounded on my high school resume. That was it. I have never really been interested in running. Nevertheless, I had to run, and running was not easy to do. My biggest problem was with pacing myself. I would start out fast, but I would end up last—or passed out on the sideline. I will never forget running in my one and only state qualifying meet. I started out running with intensity. I felt like I was going so fast the wind could not keep up with me. My bubble quickly burst when I noticed other kids passing me like speeding bullets. I went from being a close third place finish to being nearly last. I was almost out of breath. My legs hurt. My eyes hurt. I just wanted to find any reason to quit. I just kept running. The final straw came when two young women casually ran past me as they talked to one another. They were not focused on winning at all. The ease in their running angered me because I was giving everything I had. I concocted a plan to fake an injury so it would not make being last so bad after all. Upon coming up to this big tree I purposefully tripped over it and banged my leg and knee up against the roots that were protruding out of the ground. Some of my teammates who were already done with the race ran over to me. I had medical personnel out trying to assist me. It was a big deal. Although I was in last place I told everyone that I wanted to cross the finish line. I hobbled my way through the finish line with people standing on the sidelines cheering for me. My plan worked—

kind of. I was not really supposed to get hurt, but I did. That was my last race that year. Nevertheless, the moral of the story was about pacing ourselves. I did not pace myself like I should have.

When I run now I love to watch the people in the front run with intensity and energy. They are so excited they run without really thinking about the entire race. Wisdom tells me to run at a steady pace. It never fails that I always end up passing the most energetic of runners towards the middle of the race once their energy has waned. This same principle applies to the race of faith we run. It is not a sprint; it is a constant jog. We have to know the elements of distraction will try to detour us from the race. This is why we must stay focused on the end goal. Specifically, we have to fix our eyes on Jesus, the finisher of our faith.

There is another great aspect about running that differs from walking. That difference is found in the speed. Once you have found the faith to run, things that at one time distracted you when you were walking will no longer move you. You will have matured beyond the elements of distraction that come from walking alone. You will have to experience a whole new set of difficulties unique to running. Because speed is involved, there is greater risk of injury in running than there is in walking. Running also means you must have a more keen sense of vision. You cannot afford to miss the things that could cause you to stumble when you are running.

I have run before and did not pay attention to the stick lying in my path. Let's say it does not feel good when your face makes impact with the concrete. There really is no way to laugh it off. It hurts both emotionally and physically. We have all seen people fall down while running many times, in some way or another. For example, I have known men to fall by the distraction of women, drugs, sex, and even food. Their fall hurt them and the people around them. It was not pretty at all. It destroyed their family, friends, job and career. In many cases, it ruined their lives. They were out running, but were not focused on Christ. They got distracted by temptation, and fell down hard. There is only one way to go after you have fallen and that is back on your feet. The process of getting back to your feet is not as easy as it sounds. Some can pop back up quicker than others. For some it even takes some years. And there are some who never quite make it back up. They grow content with being on the ground. The difficulty comes in because of the damage made on impact. Remember the damage suffered is not just physical; it is also emotional. The damage of losing your family and friends can be more than a man is willing to handle even though his actions were the cause of it all. The guilt and shame will weigh on him so much he will not want to get back up on his feet.

I have known the faith it takes to walk and run, and both are substantial. They both take everything you have in order to accomplish the goal. And one has not finished walking or running until he has taken his final breath.

I would like to think I garnered the faith to run with passion and enthusiasm when I resigned from my last job. That was an event I will never forget and one that I am enthusiastic about sharing with you in hopes it will encourage you to obey God no matter the circumstances. Use my testimony to encourage you.

After dropping out of college I moved back to my parent's home. I went from being independent to dependent. The only difference from the past was that my dependence was on God more than it was my parents. I spent hours in prayer daily. I also worked out at the gym to curb the energy that raged within my body. I had a desire to stay active, but God was calling me to a special time of rest. After hours of prayer and weeping God would tell me to be patient and rest. That was His response to many questions for more than year. I began to grow weary as I watched my former classmates excel in school. I felt like I was missing out on something. I felt like I was being robbed of an opportunity to enjoy my youthfulness. I found myself confined to my closet for hours.

After a year of asking God to use me for His will and allow me to get active, He answered me in more ways than one. I used my downtime to pray and seek His face. I had to learn the necessity and power in prayer. I saw it as a means to something greater instead of seeing it for what it is—the greatest form of heartfelt communication with God and the fighting mechanism for every believer. Nevertheless, my prayer for more activity was answered. I received a call from my pastor at that time, and he told me God told him I was supposed to work for him. I was not excited about the news because I did not want to work for a church. Although I knew I was being groomed as a preacher I did not want to do it. I wanted to stay as far away from the pulpit as I possibly could. I just did not want the title or responsibility. I was only twenty years old at the time. I was inexperienced and very immature. Many wanted the position, but it was only offered to me. Many see being close to the pastor as a great position. Unfortunately, I did not really understand the magnitude and the depth of responsibility of the position. All I wanted was for God to make me active in His will. What I got was something much better, and I am thankful for the opportunity. Here is the rest of this story.

I agreed to go in to the office the next day and see if I was correct in saying I would not work for a church. The job was to be the pastor's personal assistant. I did not truly understand the responsibility it came with at the time. As I stated, I was very immature and inexperienced. All I knew was God confirmed to me it was the job I was supposed to take. I did not ask for it. I did not put in a resume for it. I did not inquire about it. In fact, the job was not posted anywhere. No one could apply. The only way anyone would have known about it was to speak directly with the pastor himself. He wanted God to instruct him on who he should hire, and I was the person selected.

The job took more out of me than I could have ever anticipated. It forced me to focus on details, which is not my strongest quality. I like to think that I am better with a big picture than looking at details. The job forced me to be disciplined; to mature; to truly focus on my work. The natural components of the job were very demanding. The emotional and spiritual aspects were even more demanding. I was twenty years old when I started working at the church. I did not have any real office work experience besides a short summer internship at CNN. I did not have a college degree to boast or brag on. I had no formal training on assisting anyone. All I could do was rely on the Holy Spirit for guidance and strength.

The emotional and spiritual toll was at times more than what I was willing to pay. Being around the pastor is a precious position. The pastor I worked for did not have a small church. His churches and offices spanned the world. His television broadcast was in every major outlet one could think of. He covered a lot of local networks as well. The job was not a small one at all. I look back and I am astonished God wanted me to do it. However, I know He wanted me to learn some great lessons while working there. Being around the pastor was stressful enough. Working for him was more than I could handle at times. He was very demanding of my time and energy. He did not want anything but excellence all the time. I had to learn to appreciate that quality about him. In fact, I really appreciate it now. He did not want excuses, and there was no way I could get around doing an excellent job all the time. Being human, which means I am prone to fail at times, meant nothing to him. He wanted my best at all times. When I did not deliver I was reprimanded. The emotional toll weighed so heavy on me at times. There were also times when I would barely remember driving home after a long day of work and travel. I would climb into bed late at night only to wake up early and do it all over again. You have to understand that my job was not just in the office. I traveled with him also. Being on the road made it difficult to do work back at the office, so it meant I had to work double time to complete my assignments.

I would like to think he noticed my maturity and willingness to take emotional blows from him. He noticed it by constantly giving me raises as he felt I deserved them. Honestly, the money would not prove to be enough to pay the emotional and physical toll the job was having on my body. There were times I worked some 14 to 18-hour days. Now, I have worked 23-hour days before, but it was in the food industry serving hot dogs and pretzels. That job was a little easier to manage because I did not have the feeling of being on constant surveillance to be excellent. Nevertheless, I endured the job for almost four years and I learned so much in the process.

A year before I resigned I started to grow discontent with the job. I was tired of the verbal assaults and the emotional mind games from those in the church. I felt a deeply rooted hatred growing within me for ministry and the pastoral office. I was also privy to a lot of things I just did not need to see. I would see a lot of the televised preachers who were nothing like the persona they showed on television. Their personality was polite and welcoming; the person was rude and uninviting. That was not true for all of them though. Nonetheless, the things I witnessed clouded my beautiful picture of ministry. I begged God countless times to allow me to resign. I felt like I needed to sabotage my work so I could get fired, but my boss would not fire me. There were times I wish I had been fired because the punishment was far worse than anything I could have imagined. I also began to distance myself from some of the preaching I heard. I did not necessarily agree with the theological and fundamental beliefs of the ministry, and the passion and ferocity I once gave to my work was diminishing. I was doing the church and the pastor a great disservice by staying there. My departure was greatly needed.

After almost a year of praying about being released from the job, God answered my request. While sitting in my office He told me to write up the resignation letter. I wrote it, printed it out, signed it, and handed it my pastor who was in his office working at the time. He looked at the letter, put it down, sat back in his chair, and asked me to leave the room and finish my work. For two weeks I went to work, but nothing was said about the letter. He went on like business-as-usual. My resignation was not meant to be immediate. Because of the heaviness of my job I offered to stay in the position for three months so I could train the new hire. He did not see it that way. After going in the office a week later I felt like things were a little off. His wife came in my office and thanked me for my years of service. She was always a very peaceful presence, and I was so grateful for her thanks and words of encouragement. My respect for her grew that day, and my view of her has not changed since then. Towards the end of the day the human resource director came in my office. She and I never really saw eye-to-eye on anything, so I felt like she was going to get a kick out of being the one to tell me I was being let go early. The big smile on her face gave it away. It did not take her long to tell me my resignation was accepted and I was being released that day. She gave me a short timeframe to get my things and leave the premises. It stung deep for me because I felt like I gave my heart and soul to my job only to be asked to leave in what I felt was a demeaning way. I got my things, said my few goodbyes, and I left the premises. I slept for what felt like days once I got home. I felt a huge burden lift off my shoulders. I had relief, but I could not shake the reality that I was an unemployed man who was newly married. I did not have a lot of money in savings. Although my wife was at peace with the decision to resign, I carried the burden of it all on my shoulders. Yes, I did trust in the Lord and lean on Him, but it did not shake the uneasiness I felt. It was after my resignation that I received my next set of instructions to move to Jackson, Mississippi.

Leaving my job was more than a simple action. It really took a lot out of me. I am a worker. I have worked since I was fifteen years old. I prided myself on being independent and responsible enough to work hard for what I needed and wanted. I hate being a burden to others. However, I had no other choice but to be obedient. Resigning from my job gave me a sense of relief in that I could focus my full attention back on the Lord. I spent so much time working that He became a distant second in my line of priorities. I went back to hours of studying and praying. I needed the Holy Spirit to teach me all the things I thought I learned before. I needed Him to cleanse all the junk I collected in my heart and show me my perverse ways. I needed that time of cleansing.

I look back on the job and I am so thankful for each and every minute of it. I am thankful for the pastor's instructions and willingness to be obedient to the Lord when He commanded him to hire me. It was on the job that I was able to learn the importance of being on time even when others are late, to do everything with a degree of excellence because it all represents our Lord, and to remain focused on the tasks I have been assigned. My observations as a worker in the church really helped me in accepting the pastoral office. I now know the importance of thanking and appreciating volunteers, never commanding anyone to do anything God has not told them to do, and never making something a requirement in the church Jesus has not made a requirement for salvation. I also learned to never grow so far away from the congregants that I no longer empathize with them. My experience while working at the church taught me the importance of endurance and doing what I have to do even though I do not want to do it. I was challenged, and I needed the challenge even though I did not understand it at the time. I will be forever grateful for it.

Now I am the pastor of a church, and I can proudly say that I am product of the Holy Spirit's teaching and leading. It does not come with a formal degree that is seen with the eyes, but it is viewable through the eyes of faith. It was in His school that I realized preachers are not formed in classrooms; they are formed in closets. He takes them in and breaks their perverse heart. He pulls out of them all the stuff that is not like Him. He teaches them His ways and tests them accordingly. It is no walk in the park. It is more intense than any class I have ever taken, and the cool thing about it is the classes do not end until the student takes his final breath. There is always something new to learn and more to share.

Dropping out of college definitely lessened the fear of resigning from my job, but it did not curb all the anxiety. I still had a lot of critics who felt as if their opinions mattered. I had to make sure they understood I did not ask them for their opinion before I make my decisions, and I was not interested in hearing it afterwards either. Because my position was coveted by many they saw my departure as a way for them to gain the position for themselves. Many of my so-called friends and acknowledged enemies saw my departure as an opportunity to ruin my name and reputation. Many did not know what happened with the job because I did not make it public. They had no substantial proof, so they came up with their own ideas. I saw it as a waste of time to try to refute them. Giving a clown a stage only means you desire to watch them perform. I just do not have time to buy tickets to a drama show. My wife and I were called all sorts of names. Leaders at the church instructed some we knew not to associate with us. We were considered the "prodigal children." Failure was supposed to be our outcome. What they did not realize was that with God we could not fail. There was no way they could curse those God had already blessed and anointed.

Leaving the job did take a lot out of me, but it taught me so much about the life of faith. One of the most amazing lessons I learned was I could not stay in a position just because of the way it looked to others. My position was very attractive. I had a good salary for a kid with no college degree. I lived alone in a nice two-story home. I had the things most of my peers where working hard to attain. I flew around on private jets and ate at the best restaurants. I sat on the front row and was given preferential treatment. Most called me a fool to walk away from the glamor of the position, but I could not afford to stay there just for the look of it. I had to be obedient to God. I could not allow the salary to keep me either.

Before leaving my job my wife's faith was put to the test. She lived in New York at the time and she was working for a great company on Wall Street. Many told us we should not get married until she found a job in Atlanta. Our faith told us otherwise. I called Heather one day and told her to go to her boss and explain to her that she was getting married and moving to Atlanta. God assured me He would make everything work together for His good. Although apprehensive, my wife told her boss everything. The boss offered my wife to keep her job. She would allow her to work as a contractor. She could keep her regular pay and work from home in Atlanta. There was no way my wife as going to be able to find a job with the pay she was making in Atlanta, and I was adamant about not having her to work at the church. God once again proved Himself to be faithful, if only we would step out in faith.

My wife and I have many friends who have taken similar steps of faith. Many of them followed the voice of God when He told them to leave their jobs. Today they have thriving businesses. They are able to commit more time to their family and give more to their church and community. It requires a great level of discipline, but they have proven themselves to be faithful time and time again. Plus, they have engaged a very sacred principle that I wholeheartedly believe and live by: *God honors those who honor Him.* God is truly honoring them right now. It is amazing to watch.

Please do not take my testimonies of resignation and dropping out of college to mean that you should do it as well. The point of all of this is to encourage you to obey God. It is to encourage you to begin to crawl by faith, then walk, then run. I will admit I was a young man when I did these things. I had youthful vigor on my side. I was a fresh eighteen year old when I dropped out of college. I was twenty when I started working at the church. I was twenty-three when I got married, and I was twenty-four when I resigned from my job. It is amazing to look back over it all now. All of the tests and trials have proven to be worth what it cost. There is nothing in this world that could ever outdo God's faithfulness and offering pure obedience to Him. Continue to seek Him and find the courage to run.

10

Beckoned Me to Him

How great a God we serve that He graciously guides us to Himself. I am constantly reminded that everything I do is for His glory. The sacrifice on the cross was for His glory. The redemption of His people was for His glory. Every service and action taken by His people is for His glory. The expansion of the church is for His glory. Everything we have and are belong to Him. It is all for His glory. It brings tears of joy to my eyes to know He did not and has not left us.

We, as believers, are beckoned to faith. It is a high requirement of all of us. We do not merely believe on our own. It is God who opens our blinded eyes as we read in Psalm 146:8. We also have a great illustration of this truth in Matthew 9:28-31. Jesus entered the house of blind men, and He asked them if they believed He was able to open their blinded eyes. After affirming that they did believe, He opened their eyes according to their faith. Jesus does not just heal physical blindness; He also heals spiritual blindness as well. Jesus also confirmed

Himself as Lord in John 9:35-39. Such confirmation drives spiritual blindness and grants salvation by faith. However, we know our faith does not lie dormant. James writes in James 2:17 that "Even so faith, if it have not works, is dead in itself." The faith that grants us salvation through and in Jesus cannot lie dead in the four walls of the church. It does not stand on the corner of the city block. It does not sit for an hour in the pews or solely stand for an hour in the pulpit. Our faith does not sit idly in a choir robe waiting for the next song to sing. Our faith has life, and the life of our faith is proven in our actions. Our acts of giving, praying, fasting, loving, resisting, and honoring are proof our faith is sure. Faith does not go to be received by the shaking of the pastor's hand nor is it fulfilled in a repeat-after-me prayer on a Sunday afternoon at the close of an emotional service. True faith is imputed from God and is seen in our daily activities where we honor Him by walking in spiritual truths and obeying Him at His every command. Faith is more than just taking the next step without seeing the staircase. It is being willing to reconstruct the entire staircase and build it in the way God commands if the task called for it. This is the faith we embody. This is the faith we believe. This is the faith we have been beckoned to.

"Amazing Grace" is a wonderful song many have sung for years. I particularly love the verse that speaks of the eyes of the blind being opened. It warms my soul to know God is not just sitting idly by waiting for us to come to Him. He is beckoning us to come. We are not the initiators in our relationship with Him. He first summons us and opens our blinded eyes. He first loved us before we ever thought anything good of Him. He first sent Jesus to die for our sins while we were yet unworthy of such an act. Can you fathom that truth? Does that not bring tears to your eyes to know eternal life has been granted to you because of the Christ? Have our hearts become so hardened by worldly influence we no longer consider these simple truths and take time to actually meditate on God's goodness and mercy? Where would you be if it had not been for Christ? You should rejoice and be thankful. Your thankfulness should overflow into passion and such passion should overflow into preaching.

This is why the Gospel is called Good News. It is good news we have been saved by grace and faith through Jesus. That is very good news. I am convinced many do not grasp or understand the good news because they are unaware of the bad news. The bad news is those who are without Christ will suffer eternal punishment and hell. They will inherit death and all that goes along with it. Their punishment will be harsh. That is the bad news. Those of us who have been beckoned to Christ will not suffer that pain and we will not experience that death.

We must recognize we do not serve a passive God; therefore, we are not granted a passive faith. Those who are beckoned to Him are able to freely approach His throne of grace and live out the very truths written in Scripture. We, like our great cloud of witnesses, understand that faith breeds action. Noah had to employ his faith to build an ark. Abraham had to employ his faith to sacrifice his son. Moses had to employ his faith to lead the people of Israel out of Egypt. Paul had to employ his faith to leave his intellectualism and prideful life behind to graciously follow Christ. Peter had to employ his faith to leave his profession behind of catching fish so he could be trained on how to catch men for Christ. Our faith does not stay dormant. It lives. It must live.

It is not a light matter to be beckoned by God. It will require great sacrifice. I would ask for you not to believe the lies of the ages that you are supposed to live your best life now. The best life we live is not now; our best life is what is to come. Our life of faith here on earth is filled with tests and trials. We are called to endure and work. When we are constantly focused on eternal life with Christ then this world as we know it does not compare to what is to come. Our life of faith will not look like that of the world. We will be asked to do things that astonish worldly minds. We will be misunderstood. We will be different. However, that is what we have been called to do. No believer should strive to have worldly success—which is the accumulation and love of money and things. Instead, we are called to be successful by being obedient to all God has commanded.

We are being beckoned to seek Him daily. He desires to reveal Himself to us. Have you cried out to Him as an act of faith that proves you actually believe He will do as He has said? Have you given up the idea of what you think your life should be or how it should look?

I never would have thought I would be doing what I am doing now as an author, international speaker, or businessman as a profession. Preaching is not my profession; it is my passion. I did not think this was possible for me. Politics was my passion and the White House was my goal. I viewed the work of a preacher as a worthless pursuit. However, I relinquished all rights to my life. I became a bond slave to Christ. My life is no longer my own. He has full rights to it. My objective now is to be obedient to all He commands for me to do. I do not understand how a person of faith can say he has life all figured out. As for me, I do not have it figured out at all. I am still trying to understand it. I do know my goal is to remain focused on hearing all God tells me to do and not be distracted. The same goes for you. Do not think God's beckoning is the end for you. In fact, it is only the beginning. There is still so much work that is to be done.

11

The Conclusion of the Matter

I look back over my life and I can see God's work in and around me. As you have read, my life has not been conventional. I have not taken what is perceived as a normal route. I have been laughed at, persecuted, and questioned time and time again. But, I have also been humbled, blessed, and honored for my willingness to walk by faith.

I am reminded of my courting relationship with my wife. Choosing not to kiss her until marriage was an act of my faith. I believed that by honoring her I would be honoring God. And I truly believed that if I honored God, He would honor me.

I am reminded of our wedding ceremony. We did not have a lot of money to spend. All we had was faith. We believed that God would honor our sacrifice and honor towards Him. We were able to pay for our entire wedding without having to borrow from anyone. The total was close to $30,000. Many of our friends chose different routes. They placed their faith in people or banking institutions only to be discouraged time and time again. Our faith was sufficient, and God honored it.

I am reminded of when we needed to move to another place while we lived in Mississippi. Nothing we looked at was sufficient. However, we believe God sent someone to tell us about a property that worked out to be perfect for what we wanted. And it cost much less than what we had anticipated spending. Our faith was sufficient, and God honored it.

I am reminded of our desire to have a child. I remember the day in the doctor's office when he told us there was no heartbeat and the baby will be miscarried. I remember the emotions we felt that day. I remember the anger and pain that raged in my heart. I remember the desire to quit God and deny Him because I could not understand why He would not give us a child. I did not understand why the miscarriage had to happen. But we chose to remain faith-filled. We chose to continue to call on God and trust He would provide when He felt was best. On March 13, 2013, my wife gave birth to a healthy boy we named Logan William Lindsey. After almost a year and a half of praying and staying faithful, we were honored with a child. Our faith was sufficient, and God honored it.

I am reminded of January 26, 2013 when we opened The Gathering Oasis Church in Atlanta, Georgia. As I stepped on the platform to preach I looked out in the audience to over 600 people for our very first service. The numbers have fluctuated since then, but I could not believe my eyes. I have heard stories of churches starting in living rooms and libraries. I was humbled by the attendance on that first Sunday. I remember thanking God for His grace and faithfulness. I remember the day He told me to open His church. I remember the nights I woke up from having dreams about His church. I remember the day He gave me specifics about what we should do with the church. I remember it so well. I was fearful and apprehensive. But I believed my honor towards God in obedience would reciprocate His honor towards me. I chose to believe He would provide and take care of everything by faith. Since then, the church has never missed payments and has been able to operate with a surplus—no matter how small. He has been faithful. My faith was sufficient, and God honored it.

I could go on and on and on with stories about how God honored His word. The conclusion of the matter is this: fear God and remain in faith. Do not become so friendly with our holy God you lose all respect for Him. Honor and revere Him. Obey quickly when He commands you. Do not look to the left or right. Do not be distracted. Like Abraham, be willing to leave behind your family, native land, and ruling order so you can go to a place God will show you. Like Abraham, be willing to sacrifice what is precious to you. Like Job, never allow your current situation to define your argument against or for God. Remain faithful no matter the level of difficulty. Do not think everything should go your way or the way you picture it. Just remain faithful. Like David, have courage to stand up to the adversary no matter how big it may appear. Be wiling to be courageous. Like Joseph, do not allow anyone to tell you what God has revealed to you is not true. Do not allow their disbelief to kill your faith. Stand firm in the face of opposition and keep your eyes on the crown that is earned by those who endure this trial-filled life. Like Joshua, be willing to take the land that was promised to you. Let nothing or no one stand in your way. Like Jesus, be humble and submissive. Do not attempt to subvert your will or authority over anyone. Deny yourself and your worldly cravings so you are able to please God and honor every word He gives.

Stand in faith. Walk in faith. Run in faith. Live in faith. It is by faith that we are able to please God. Do not stop. You must endure. The crowning achievement of your life will not be the amount of stuff you were able to accumulate. Your success as a believer will not be how high you were able to climb at your job, the number of degrees you were able to obtain, or the number of cars you were able to put in your driveway. Your success will come from your ability to walk by faith and remain obedient to all God has commanded of you. It is impossible for you to properly obey God without faith. Do not ignore the conviction that is in your heart right now. You know the steps you should take. You know the path He has placed you on. Do not ignore it. You must walk by faith. You must step out of your comfort zone and risk being uncomfortable. In fact, you must become comfortable with being uncomfortable. It is time to act. It is time to move. It is time to walk by faith.

16079068R00060

Made in the USA
Middletown, DE
04 December 2014